Original title:
Dreamy Drifts and Starry Shifts

Copyright © 2024 Creative Arts Management OÜ
All rights reserved.

Author: Clara Whitfield
ISBN HARDBACK: 978-9916-90-504-3
ISBN PAPERBACK: 978-9916-90-505-0

When Stars Paint the Sky with Hope

In twilight's embrace, dreams take flight,
Stars sprinkle wishes, glimmering bright.
Each twinkle a promise, a soft-spoken tale,
Whispers of hope in the cool night gale.

The canvas of sky, a masterpiece grand,
Brushstrokes of light from a cosmic hand.
Hearts are ignited, shadows take flight,
When stars paint the sky, all feels right.

The Symphony of Starlight and Silence

In the quiet of night, the cosmos sings,
A symphony woven with delicate strings.
Each star a note in the vast, dark sea,
Harmony flows, setting the spirit free.

Silence amplifies the celestial score,
Echoes of wonders, always wanting more.
Lost in the melody, time stands still,
As starlight dances with a soft, gentle thrill.

Evocations from Beyond the Veil

Murmurs of the past in the mist arise,
Echoes of laughter beneath ancient skies.
The veil is thin where whispers convene,
Ghosts of the memories, forever unseen.

In shadows that flicker, stories unfold,
Tales of the brave, of the lost and bold.
Winds carry secrets, the night gently sways,
In evocations from timeless ways.

A Flight through Sonic Dreamscapes

On wings of sound, we soar through the night,
Colors of music, vivid and bright.
Each note a feather, light as the air,
Carving through silence, a journey rare.

In dreamscapes alive, where echoes play,
Melodies whisper and softly sway.
A tapestry woven of rhythm and rhyme,
In a flight through horizons outside of time.

The Silent Art of Cosmic Wandering

In the hush of night, stars unfold,
Whispers of dreams in silver and gold.
Galaxies dance in a waltz so grand,
A canvas of wonders, time's gentle hand.

Comets pass by with tales to share,
Of worlds unseen and cosmic prayer.
Each heartbeat echoes through the vast sea,
A silent art in which we roam free.

Floating on the Fabric of the Unknown

Drifting through realms where shadows play,
Threads of fate woven night and day.
Clouds of thought in endless flight,
A tapestry stitched with dreams of light.

In the silence, we find our way,
Floating gently, come what may.
The unknown whispers secrets sweet,
In every journey, life's heartbeat.

Sketches of Past and Future Dreams

With a pen made of stardust, I draw the past,
Moments that linger, memories that last.
Future horizons call out my name,
Sketches of dreams set the heart aflame.

Each line a pathway, twists and turns,
Lessons learned as the soul yearns.
In every scribble, stories unfold,
The past and the future in one hand to hold.

Wishes Carried on Midnight Breezes

On midnight winds, wishes take flight,
Soft as a whisper, bright as the night.
Carried to heavens where hopes find peace,
In the stillness, a moment of release.

Stars listen closely to hearts that yearn,
Each flicker of light, a wish we discern.
In the quiet, our dreams intertwine,
Wishes on breezes, your soul and mine.

Ethereal Odyssey on Softest Winds

On gentle gusts, we sail away,
Through whispered dreams, where shadows play.
The clouds adorn a sapphire hue,
In realms of light, where wishes grew.

With every breath, the stars align,
A symphony of dreams, divine.
Soft melodies embrace the night,
As we drift towards the morning light.

Whispers of Celestial Waves

The ocean sings in murmurs sweet,
A lullaby where starlight meets.
Ripples dance under moonlit grace,
Caressing shores, a soft embrace.

Each wave a tale of love retold,
In whispers deep, a heart of gold.
Reflections shimmer on the tide,
As secrets in the currents glide.

Fantasia in Midnight Tides

Beneath the moon, the waters gleam,
A fantasy, an endless dream.
The night unfolds its velvet hand,
Inviting souls to drift and stand.

With every splash, a story's spun,
Mysteries of the night begun.
In twilight's arms, we find our place,
As stars pirouette in silent grace.

Cosmic Quills on Velvet Sky

With cosmic quills, the night is drawn,
A tapestry of dusk till dawn.
Galaxies swirl in colors bright,
As dreams take flight on wings of light.

The velvet sky, a canvas wide,
Where wishes ride the stellar tide.
In every spark, a tale to tell,
As hearts unite in magic's spell.

Cosmic Reveries and Celestial Breezes

Stars whisper softly in the night,
Galaxies dance, a delicate light.
Echoes of dreams in endless flight,
Caught in the cosmos, pure delight.

Nebulas swirl in vivid streams,
Woven with magic, spun from dreams.
A tapestry bright, or so it seems,
Breezes of wonder, timeless themes.

Celestial Dreams in a Midnight Haze

Moonlight drapes the world in silver,
As shadows flicker, soft and shiver.
Whispers of worlds where spirits quiver,
Floating on currents of the river.

Stars ignite thoughts in twilight's embrace,
Lighting the path to a sacred place.
Each sigh of night lends time a grace,
In celestial dreams, our hearts we trace.

Voyage Through the Echoes of Elysium

Sailing through thoughts in a starlit sea,
Echoes of laughter, wild and free.
In every wave, a memory,
Of love and hope, eternity.

Celestial shores, where spirits glide,
Underneath skies, vast and wide.
In the breeze, let your heart confide,
As the universe swells with pride.

Chasing Shadows Beneath the Northern Lights

Beneath the glow, shadows intertwine,
As auroras dance, a celestial sign.
Hearts beat in rhythm, pure and divine,
Chasing the wonders, your hand in mine.

Whispers of magic on frosted air,
Weaving through darkness, pure and rare.
In this embrace, we lay our care,
Chasing the shadows, a love to share.

Gossamer Threads of Night

In the cloak of dusk we weave,
Dreams suspended, hearts believe,
Whispers soft on silken air,
Gossamer threads that shimmer fair.

Stars peek through the velvet blue,
Each a secret, ancient, true,
In this tapestry of time,
We find solace in the rhyme.

Moonlight dances on the ground,
In the silence, peace is found,
Gentle echoes, shadows play,
Guiding us through night to day.

Held within the night's embrace,
We discover, we trace,
Threads of light, a glowing spark,
In the end, we'll leave our mark.

Embracing the Unknown in Stillness

Amidst the quiet, thoughts unfold,
The unknown whispers, brave and bold,
We stand at edges, hearts aligned,
In stillness, new paths we find.

Unraveled fears in shadows cast,
Embracing moments, holding fast,
With every breath, the world expands,
In gentle silence, life commands.

Hesitations drift like leaves,
In the still air, hope believes,
We journey forth, though blind we walk,
In the quiet, courage talks.

Life awaits, with arms outspread,
In the unknown, dreams are bred,
So let us breathe, let go, be free,
In stillness lies the key to see.

Starlight Whispering Secrets of Infinity

In the depths of the midnight sky,
Stars unfold their tales on high,
Each spark a whisper, secrets shared,
In the cosmos, we are bared.

Galaxies spin, a dance divine,
Time and space, a woven line,
In their glow, we seek our place,
Amongst the void, in vast embrace.

Lightyears echo, stories told,
Galactic dreams, both new and old,
As we linger, breathless, still,
Starlight beckons, hearts to fill.

Embracing wonders, free and bright,
Whispers carried on winds of night,
In the great expanse, we find our way,
Secrets of infinity, come what may.

Reflections in a Cosmos of Wishes

In the mirror of the night, we see,
Reflections glimmer, wild and free,
Each wish a star, a little bright,
Floating gently through the night.

Fractals dance in cosmic streams,
Colorful echoes of our dreams,
As we reach for hopes so wide,
In this universe, we confide.

Moments flicker, timeless grace,
In the silence, we find our place,
Every heartbeat, a wish expressed,
In this cosmos, we're truly blessed.

Boundless skies first light our goals,
Connecting hearts, igniting souls,
Wishes reflect in every glance,
Carried on the night's romance.

Night's Embrace on a Galactic Canvas

Beneath the stars, whispers arise,
Veils of darkness, twinkling ties.
Dreams awaken in shadowed air,
As night unfolds its silent care.

Galaxies spin in quiet dance,
Each a spark in a timeless trance.
Painted skies of deep azure hues,
A cosmic hug, a gentle muse.

Moonlight drapes like silken threads,
Where secrets linger, softly spread.
Each moment stretched, a breath in space,
Night's embrace, a warm embrace.

In this vastness, we are small,
Yet find our place, a sacred call.
The universe, a canvas wide,
Night's embrace, our hearts collide.

The Poetry of a Wistful Sky

Clouds drift softly, dreams in flight,
Colors blending, day turns night.
Whispers carried on the breeze,
Emotions dance with such great ease.

Stars peek out, shy yet bright,
A tapestry of twinkling light.
Each a story, calm and clear,
The sky's poetry draws us near.

Wistful sighs of fading day,
Hints of twilight in bright array.
Crimson blush, a painter's hue,
Sky's soft verse speaks deep and true.

In every shade, a tale unfolds,
Romance written in orange and gold.
A sonnet shared with every sigh,
The poetry of a wistful sky.

Celestial Quest of the Wandering Heart

Underneath the cosmic veil,
A heart wanders, bold yet frail.
Chasing dreams on starlit seas,
With every pulse, the spirit frees.

Galactic paths, a course unknown,
To distant worlds, the heart is drawn.
Finding solace in the night,
Guided by the silver light.

Each twinkle beckons, softly calls,
To rise above the earthly walls.
Adventurous souls, forever roam,
In the universe, they find their home.

A quest that spans both time and space,
In every corner, a hidden place.
The wandering heart, relentless and true,
Seeks the heavens, forever new.

Embracing the Silence Between Stars

In the hush where shadows lie,
Quiet moments drift and sigh.
Stars converse in glowing breath,
Embracing silence, defying death.

Galaxies breathe, a tranquil sound,
In the void, peace is found.
Crickets chirp in cosmic tones,
The universe hums, no need for phones.

Between each star, a pause remains,
A gentle calm that soothes the pains.
In vast expanse, we find our way,
Embracing silence, the night's ballet.

In every heartbeat, there is grace,
As time slips softly through this space.
We find our truth, our guiding scars,
In silence sweet, between the stars.

Surrender to the Softness of Night

Beneath the cloak of twilight,
Soft whispers cradle the day.
Moonbeams dance on gentle waves,
As stars begin their quiet play.

Shadows stretch across the land,
Embracing all in velvet peace.
The world holds its breath in awe,
In this moment, time finds release.

Crickets serenade the night,
Their songs like secrets in the air.
Each sigh of wind a lullaby,
Inviting hearts to linger there.

Close your eyes, let worries fade,
In this stillness find your flight.
Surrender to the magic here,
And drift into the softest night.

Horizons Where Dreams Kiss the Sky

At dawn, horizons come alive,
Where colors blend, and spirits soar.
A canvas vast, where dreams take flight,
And hearts wander forevermore.

Golden rays break through the dark,
Touched by hope, they warm the ground.
In this moment, visions spark,
As whispered wishes swirl around.

Clouds adorned with silver seams,
Echo promises of what could be.
Chase the pathways born from dreams,
And let your spirit fly so free.

Horizons stretch beyond our hands,
Embracing futures yet to find.
In the light where dreams hold hands,
Life's endless stories intertwine.

Caressed by Celestial Zephyrs

In twilight's hush, we are embraced,
By gentle winds that weave through trees.
They carry secrets, soft and light,
Caressing us like whispered pleas.

Stars above, like diamonds bright,
Twinkle softly, guiding our way.
We dance beneath their watchful eyes,
And drift on zephyrs, come what may.

Each breeze a touch, each sigh a song,
In this embrace, we find our place.
Lost in time, we journey long,
To dance with dreams in boundless space.

Let go of fears, let spirit soar,
On wings of night, we'll glide and twirl.
Caressed by breezes, evermore,
In the embrace of night's soft swirl.

Mosaic of Starlight Dreams

In the velvet of the night,
A mosaic built from dreams takes form.
Every star a secret bright,
Illuminating paths to warm.

We gather pieces of the sky,
Fragments of hopes and whispered wishes.
Through these shards, our spirits fly,
In the tapestry of celestial dishes.

Light spills forth from every seam,
Weaving stories, vibrant and rare.
In this realm, we hold our dream,
And find our joy suspended in air.

Together in this starlit dance,
Each moment glows, each heartbeat sings.
In this mosaic, we find our chance,
To soar on love's enchanted wings.

Whispers of Twilight's Embrace

In the hush of twilight's glow,
Soft whispers dance, gentle and slow.
Stars awaken in velvet skies,
As secrets murmur, truth underlies.

The breeze carries tales untold,
Of dreams and wishes, brave and bold.
Crickets serenade the night,
Nature's symphony, pure delight.

Shadows lengthen, merging hues,
With every whisper, the heart renews.
A moment frozen, time stands still,
In twilight's embrace, we find our will.

With each breath, the magic weaves,
A tapestry of hope, as the heart believes.
In this twilight, love takes flight,
Whispers echo in the fading light.

Celestial Tides and Luminous Glides

Beneath the moon's soft, silver glow,
The ocean dances, ebbing slow.
Celestial tides with mystique abound,
In luminous glides, our spirits are found.

Stars cascade like dreams alight,
Guiding the lost through tranquil night.
The waves whisper secrets, old as time,
In harmony, our hearts will chime.

Each ripple holds a tale to share,
Of wanderers lost, of love laid bare.
Embracing the cosmos, vast and wide,
We find ourselves in the celestial tide.

Through night's embrace, we drift and glide,
In unison with the world, side by side.
With every breath, we rise and fall,
In nature's rhythm, we hear the call.

Nightfall's Gentle Caress

The sun dips low, a fiery ray,
Nightfall whispers, softly at play.
Stars emerge, a jeweled crown,
Night's gentle touch, in silence, drowns.

Shadows blend with twilight's grace,
In the stillness, we find our place.
A calm descends, fears dissipate,
With night's embrace, we contemplate.

The world transforms, a canvas grand,
Mysteries weave, as dreams expand.
In every heartbeat, solace found,
Nightfall's tender caress surrounds.

Beneath the stars, hopes ignite,
Guided by the soft moonlight.
In this moment, all is well,
Nightfall wraps us in its spell.

Wanderlust Beneath a Cosmic Veil

Beneath a cosmic blanket bright,
Wanderers seek the endless night.
The galaxy hums a daring tune,
Underneath the watchful moon.

Hearts aflame with dreams of flight,
Exploring wonders, pure delight.
Each star a guide, a distant spark,
In this vastness, we leave our mark.

With whispered hopes, we drift and roam,
Finding joy in the unknown home.
Each step a venture through the dark,
Our wanderlust ignited, a glowing arc.

Beneath the cosmos, we dare to see,
The beauty of life's vast tapestry.
In every heartbeat, we will unveil,
The magic of nights, our cosmic trail.

In the Glow of Starlit Reverie

Underneath the velvet sky,
Whispers of the night do sigh,
Magic dances on the breeze,
Cradled in the dark with ease.

Dreamers wander, hearts in flight,
Tracing paths of twinkling light,
Moonbeams guide our secret quests,
Wrapped in warmth, the world at rest.

Lost in thoughts, we find our peace,
In gentle moments, troubles cease,
Stars above in quiet grace,
Inviting us to seek and trace.

In this glow, our spirits soar,
Seeking more, we yearn for lore,
Embrace the night, feel its call,
In the starlit reverie, we fall.

Celestial Sighs and Ephemeral Moments

In twilight's tender, fleeting breath,
We find the echoes, life's sweet depth,
Time slips gently through our hands,
Moments scattered like golden sands.

The stars above, they softly sing,
Of dreams they guard and love they bring,
Each shimmering note drifts and flies,
In harmony with celestial sighs.

Seasons dance, all transient, bright,
Fleeting beauty, day turns to night,
Capture joy with every glance,
In ephemeral moments, we take a chance.

So hold each breath, let it flow,
Worlds collide in the afterglow,
With love and light, we walk this mile,
Cherishing life's exquisite style.

A Compass for Dreamers Lost

When shadows gather, darkness looms,
Seek the light that brightly blooms,
Stars ignite the path we tread,
With a compass in our head.

Wandering hearts, we roam unknown,
In search of solace, we have grown,
Each step a story, each turn a guide,
In the labyrinth where dreams abide.

Hope lights the way through night's embrace,
With courage stitched in time and space,
A gentle whisper, trust your heart,
In this journey, we take our part.

For dreamers lost but never stray,
With every compass, find our way,
In the embrace of whispered fate,
Our dreams will chart a path so great.

Chasing Shadows of Shimmering Light

Beneath the sky where shadows play,
We chase the glimmers, night and day,
Each flicker holds a secret bright,
In the chase of shimmering light.

The dance of hues, the twilight's grace,
Reflects the dreams we long to trace,
With every breath, we dive and leap,
Into the depths, our souls to keep.

Measured in moments, we embark,
Filling our lives with every spark,
In whispered hues, our hearts ignite,
To turn the shadows into light.

As daylight fades, don't lose the thrill,
Chase the shadows, seek the still,
In this journey, let love be bright,
Forever chasing, day and night.

Songs of the Celestial Wanderers

Whispers drift through endless skies,
Shooting stars in silent cries.
Galaxies twirl in a cosmic dance,
Echoes of a timeless romance.

Constellations tell their tales,
Of love that journeys, never pales.
In the void where shadows play,
Wanderers seek the light of day.

Each twinkle holds a cherished wish,
A glimpse of fate in the starlit swish.
Through the dark, their spirits soar,
Finding peace forevermore.

In the vastness, hearts align,
Lost in space, but never blind.
Songs of wanderers fill the air,
A melody of dreams laid bare.

Fires of the Cosmic Heart

Within the depths of night's embrace,
Burn the embers of endless space.
Galactic flames ignite the night,
A blaze of love, a beacon bright.

Comets streak with fiery tails,
Carrying hopes that never fails.
In the dark, the heartbeats thrum,
An orchestra of worlds to come.

Each spark a story, fierce and bold,
In the silence, heat takes hold.
Celestial fires, warm and grand,
United, the cosmos takes a stand.

Through the void, the flames will rise,
Enkindling dreams in midnight skies.
Fires of the heart, forever free,
A testament to what can be.

Serenes of Solstice and Dreams

When shadows dance 'neath the pale moonlight,
Serenity blooms in the quiet night.
Solstice whispers through the trees,
Where dreams take flight on gentle breeze.

Stars align in a celestial glow,
Guiding hearts where the currents flow.
Embracing peace as time stands still,
In the stillness, the world will heal.

Through twilight's veil, our spirits weave,
The tapestry of what we believe.
In the stillness, hopes remain,
As we gather strength through joy and pain.

In the wake of dawn, we rise anew,
Chasing visions, daring to pursue.
Serenes of life, both soft and bright,
Igniting passion with morning light.

Stardust Paths through the Veil of Night

Follow the trails of stardust dreams,
Winding through the cosmos' seams.
Each step reveals a hidden way,
Guiding souls to the break of day.

Through the veil of night so deep,
The universe sings us to sleep.
Echoes of light, softly breathe,
In the darkness, we weave and seethe.

Galaxies spin like whispered tales,
Carried on cosmic winds and gales.
With every heartbeat, we ignite,
The dance of stardust, pure and bright.

Together we tread on paths unknown,
With spirits wild and hearts of stone.
In the night, our dreams take flight,
Through stardust paths, we seek the light.

Driftwood of Time and Thought

Waves crash softly on the shore,
Whispers of old dreams once more.
Fragments of stories, lost and found,
Driftwood speaks in silence, profound.

Carried by currents, we float along,
Memories echo in a gentle song.
Years slip by like sand in hand,
Time drifts on, unclaimed, unplanned.

Moments collide in the tide's embrace,
Each piece a tale, a fleeting trace.
Thoughts adrift in the ocean's heart,
Boundless journeys, a brand new start.

In twilight's glow, we're set adrift,
Guided by stars, our spirits lift.
Such is the dance of time and thought,
In patterns woven, we've always sought.

Enchanted Echoes Beneath the Cosmos

Underneath the starlit dome,
Soft whispers call us from our home.
In silence deep, we hear the sound,
Of dreams and wishes swirling round.

Galaxies hum a timeless tune,
As night unfolds, we gaze at the moon.
Magic lingers in the air,
In every heartbeat, a cosmic flare.

Celestial wonders beckon near,
With whispered secrets we hold dear.
Beneath the vast and endless sky,
Echoes of love forever fly.

In sacred moments, we unite,
As stardust glimmers in our sight.
Together we dance, a cosmic pair,
In enchanted echoes, we are aware.

Celestial Serenades in Blue

Beneath the azure heavens high,
Melodies drift and softly sigh.
Whispers of stars in twilight's glow,
Sing of dreams that gently flow.

Notes of blue dance through the night,
Painting visions, pure and bright.
Harmony swells like ocean waves,
In every heart, a song that saves.

Celestial lights twinkle in tune,
Guiding our souls like the sun and moon.
Serenades of peace and grace,
In our spirits, they find a place.

With every breath, we play along,
In the vast expanse, we belong.
Together we sing, hand in hand,
In celestial serenades, we stand.

Shadows and Stardust in Transience

In the hush of evening's glow,
Shadows dance, soft and slow.
Time, a river, flows away,
Leaving stardust in its sway.

Fleeting moments like whispers fade,
In twilight's warmth, memories laid.
Ghostly figures in the mist,
Glimpses of a world we've kissed.

Transient dreams in the night air,
Threads of silver, tender care.
Stars appear like fleeting sighs,
Reminders of where the heart lies.

In shadows deep, we find our light,
A cosmic dance in the quiet night.
Embrace the now, let go of the past,
For shadows and stardust are meant to last.

Euphoria in the Shade of Twilight

In the soft glow of dimming light,
Whispers of dreams take gentle flight.
Stars emerge in the velvet sky,
As shadows dance and days say goodbye.

Echoes of laughter fill the air,
Moments cherished, beyond compare.
Hearts unite in the glow so bright,
Lost in the magic of the night.

Colors blend in hues of gold,
Secrets of dusk quietly unfold.
Embracing the calm, we find release,
In twilight's arms, we seize our peace.

When the Universe Takes a Breath

In stillness wrapped, the cosmos sighs,
Galaxies twinkle, painting the skies.
An infinite pause, a moment long,
Nature's heartbeat, a silken song.

Time drips slowly, like honeyed light,
We find wonder in the quiet night.
Planets cradle dreams in their spin,
In silence deep, new worlds begin.

Each star a wish, a spark, a hope,
We drift along, and learn to cope.
When the universe breathes, we too sigh,
In the embrace of the dark, we fly.

Glimmers of Solitude and Solace

In corners dim, where shadows creep,
A whispering calm begins to seep.
Solitude beckons, a gentle friend,
In its embrace, hearts can mend.

The soft rhythm of silent thoughts,
A treasure trove that time forgot.
In stillness found, reflections grow,
Glimmers of peace begin to flow.

With every breath, the world feels wide,
In quiet moments, we often hide.
Yet solitude sings a sweet refrain,
In whispers soft, amidst the pain.

Strolling Through a Universe of Illusions

Wandering paths through a maze of light,
Visions flicker in playful flight.
Mirrors tease with their mystic charms,
While dreams entwine in their gentle arms.

Every shadow holds a hidden tale,
In every glance, we briefly sail.
Phantoms dance in the moon's soft glow,
As we question what we think we know.

We chase the echoes, we laugh, we spin,
In this illusion, we lose and win.
Yet in the chaos, there's beauty's grace,
Strolling through time in this timeless space.

Slumbering Spirits and Starbound Remnants

In the quiet of night, shadows creep,
Whispers of dreams where secrets sleep.
Stars twinkle faintly, a gentle guide,
As slumbering spirits in silence abide.

Echoes of laughter from ages past,
Drifting like stardust, free and vast.
Memories woven in twilight's thread,
Filling the void where hopes once led.

Ethereal whispers call out in tune,
Beneath the gaze of a watchful moon.
Time stands still in the realms of the night,
As spirits dance in the soft, pale light.

Journey through dreams, let your soul expand,
Where starbound remnants reach out a hand.
Together they weave a celestial song,
In slumbering realms, you surely belong.

Aurora's Lullaby to Wandering Hearts

Beneath the canvas where colors flow,
Auroras sing softly, a calming glow.
Wandering hearts find solace in light,
Blessed by the beauty of the night.

Each hue a message, a tale untold,
Wrapped in warmth, as the night unfolds.
Gentle caresses from the cosmic skies,
Awakening dreams with shimmering sighs.

Drifting like feathers on whispering air,
Hearts dance together, unaware of despair.
Guided by rhythm, in peace they dwell,
Where the aurora's lullaby casts its spell.

With every twinkle, hope takes flight,
Illuminating paths in the dark of night.
Embrace the song that sings to your soul,
For wandering hearts are forever whole.

A Sojourn Through the Velvet Skies

A sojourn awaits in the velvet sprawl,
Where stars cascade and dreamers call.
On silken clouds, let your spirit soar,
In the realms of wonder, forever explore.

Hearts adrift like ships at sea,
Guided by starlight, wild and free.
Glimmers of hope in a darkened expanse,
Awakening visions in a timeless dance.

Echoes of wishes whisper through night,
Stirring the cosmos, igniting pure light.
In this boundless space, let love align,
As time unfurls in a tapestry fine.

As constellations shimmer, dreams entwine,
In velvet skies, destinies align.
Wander with courage, let your heart lead,
For in this sojourn, your soul will be freed.

Gleaming Pathways of the Ethereal Drift

Along the pathways where wonders gleam,
The ethereal drift awakens a dream.
Flickers of light guide the way ahead,
Illuminating thoughts like stars in your head.

Time flows gently through enchanted lanes,
Whispering secrets in soft refrains.
Each step you take is a dance with fate,
On pathways gleaming, hearts resonate.

Colors are woven in twilight's embrace,
As journeys unfold in this sacred space.
Lost in translation, yet feelings stay clear,
In the drift of the night, all souls hold dear.

Explore the wonders that beckon in peace,
Let the ethereal drift never cease.
For in these pathways, you'll surely find,
The dreams of the heart, unconfined.

Moonbeams Weaving Tales

In silver light, the stories dance,
Whispers carry on the breeze,
Each shimmer holds a fleeting glance,
Time pauses with such gentle ease.

Through shadows cast, the legends sing,
Of love and loss, of hopes and dreams,
With every thread, the night takes wing,
Awakening ancient, silent themes.

Beneath the glow, the secrets sway,
In tangled knots, they intertwine,
Illuminating the darkened way,
Where starlit paths and fate align.

As dawn draws near, the tales subside,
Yet echoes linger, soft and clear,
In moonbeam's grasp, hearts open wide,
Embracing all we hold so dear.

Between the Breaths of Twilight

In the hush where day meets night,
Softly whispers secrets shared,
The canvas of the fading light,
A moment grasped, a heart laid bare.

Each breath, a fleeting memory,
Caught in the dance of shadows long,
The world transforms in reverie,
Where twilight sings its sacred song.

Eyes closed, we drift through silver streams,
Tracing dreams that gently flow,
Between the breaths, our spirit gleams,
In twilight's arms, we come to know.

As stars ignite the velvet sky,
We find solace, breath by breath,
In twilight's hold, we learn to fly,
Beyond the echoes, past all death.

A Tapestry of Thoughts in Motion

In vibrant hues, the mind creates,
Weaving patterns of desire,
Emotions dance on fleeting fates,
In every thread, a spark of fire.

The colors blend, collide and sway,
A constant flow of ebbing dreams,
Thoughts spiral where the shadows play,
Reflecting all our silent screams.

With every stitch, a story grows,
A tapestry of hope and pain,
Through ups and downs, the fabric shows,
The beauty forged from love's refrain.

In motion's grasp, we thread the night,
Our hearts entwined in rhythmic pull,
Creating worlds of soft delight,
The fabric of this life, so full.

Echoes of a Fractured Cosmos

In the void where silence reigns,
Fragments dance through endless space,
Whispers of old celestial strains,
Carried forth in a dark embrace.

Stars collide in a cosmic waltz,
Each spark ignites a fiery tale,
Echoes bounce, revealing faults,
Where night conceals and dreams prevail.

Through shattered realms, new worlds emerge,
In fractured light, we find our way,
With every beat, our spirits surge,
Towards the dawn of a brand new day.

In silence deep, we hear the call,
Of galaxies both near and far,
A cosmic song that links us all,
Echoes of life beneath each star.

Mystical Currents of the Astral Sea

Waves of light dance through the night,
Guided by stars, a wondrous flight.
Celestial whispers call from afar,
A journey unfolds beneath each star.

Currents flow in silent grace,
Embracing dreams in endless space.
The universe hums with secret lore,
Inviting souls to explore and soar.

Mysteries bloom like blossoms bright,
In the depths of the cosmic light.
Galaxies swirl, a grand ballet,
As time and shadows softly sway.

Echoes of wisdom ripple wide,
In each heartbeat, the cosmos resides.
Listen closely, let your heart steer,
To the realms where all is crystal clear.

Radiance of a Nocturnal Serenade

Softly sings the moonlit sky,
As dreams and wishes tenderly vie.
Chords of night strum through the air,
A serenade of love laid bare.

Stars punctuate the velvet dome,
In this realm, we find our home.
Illuminated whispers fill the space,
Echoing softly, a warm embrace.

Between the shadows, spirits glide,
In the tranquility, they confide.
The night holds tales of ages past,
In every note, the die is cast.

Awash in melodies, hearts entwine,
In this nocturnal dance, we align.
With every breath, we rise and sway,
Lost in the magic of night's ballet.

Gossamer Visions and Galaxy Whispers

Veils of silver softly unfurl,
Dreams take flight, as thoughts swirl.
Through nebulous hues, visions glow,
In the depths of the cosmos, we flow.

Gossamer threads weave stories rare,
Galaxies murmur, secrets to share.
Between the fabric of night and day,
Whispers beckon, guiding the way.

Infinite wonders, unfathomed and vast,
In this celestial dance, we're cast.
With open hearts, we float and glide,
On the breath of the universe, we ride.

In every shimmer, a promise lies,
Under the watch of countless eyes.
Gossamer dreams whisper in our ear,
In this cosmic embrace, we have no fear.

Whirling Vortices of Stardust and Thought

Thoughts like spirals, spinning wide,
In the vortex, where dreams reside.
Stardust trails light up the night,
Guiding us through the infinite flight.

In the dance of cosmic winds,
Every moment, a new heart begins.
Whirling energies, both fierce and calm,
Cradle the spirit like a soothing balm.

Time and space twine close and tight,
In this sanctuary of pure light.
Ideas flutter, like moths to flame,
In the stardust haze, all feels the same.

We merge with the music of the spheres,
Dancing past shadows, past our fears.
In this whirlpool, we find our bliss,
A cosmic embrace, a starry kiss.

Ethereal Sojourns of the Heart

In dreams we wander, soft and light,
Where shadows bloom, and hearts take flight.
A whispered sigh, a tender glance,
In fleeting moments, we find our dance.

Beneath the stars, our spirits roam,
Through whispered woods, we find our home.
Each heartbeat echoes, wild and free,
In ethereal realms, just you and me.

The moon's embrace, it lights our way,
Through tangled paths, we dare to stay.
With every breath, our hopes entwine,
In this sojourn, your heart is mine.

So let us drift on love's soft breeze,
In timeless moments, we find our ease.
Ethereal sojourns, always near,
Forever cherished, year by year.

Luminous Winks of the Night

Stars twinkle softly, like dreams untold,
In the stillness, their magic unfolds.
With each gentle pulse, the night is alive,
Whispers of secrets, beneath the sky's dive.

Moonbeams dance on the velvet tide,
Illuminating thoughts we once tried to hide.
Luminous winks, the cosmos' delight,
Guide our hearts through the depths of the night.

Shadows of laughter, echoes of time,
Melodies linger, soft as a chime.
The world is aglow, with hopes that ignite,
In luminous winks, love takes flight.

Embrace the wonder, let passions ignite,
In the cover of darkness, we'll shine so bright.
Together we'll journey through dreams, pure and right,
Luminous winks, our hearts in the night.

Moonlit Journeys Through Celestial Depths

Under the moon's watchful embrace,
We wander far, in a timeless space.
Celestial wonders, a heart's delight,
Guiding our steps through the tranquil night.

The cosmos whispers in silken tones,
As stardust wraps us in gentle moans.
With every glance, the universe swells,
In moonlit journeys, where magic dwells.

The night unfolds like a mystic map,
In dreams we travel, no time to trap.
Every heartbeat syncs to the stars' gentle song,
In celestial depths, where we both belong.

We chase the light through the darkened skies,
In moonlit flights, where our spirit flies.
Hand in hand, we'll dare to explore,
These moonlit journeys, forever more.

When Time Slows to a Whisper

In the hush of twilight, time bends near,
Moments suspended, crystalline clear.
Every heartbeat becomes a soft tune,
As silence wraps us, like the glow of the moon.

We breathe in the calm, let the world fade,
In this sacred space, memories parade.
When time slows to whisper, love feels so vast,
Each second lingers, forever to last.

With every glance, the universe slows,
In the soft twilight, our magic glows.
In quiet stillness, our dreams intertwine,
When time slows to a whisper, your heart next to mine.

Moments unhurried, a timeless embrace,
In the dance of our souls, we find our place.
When time slows to whisper, we choose to stay,
In the heart of stillness, we'll find our way.

Starlit Journeys of the Soul

Beneath the stars, our dreams take flight,
Whispers of the night, soft and light.
The cosmos calls with a gentle sway,
Leading our hearts on a timeless way.

Through galaxies where shadows play,
The essence of us learns to sway.
In the starlit dark, we dance and roam,
Finding in the void, we are home.

Each twinkle holds a story told,
In the silence, our secrets unfold.
With every step on this astral sea,
We find the depths of our own key.

With stardust woven in our veins,
We embrace the night, releasing chains.
Together we wander, souls entwined,
In the cosmic tapestry, we find.

Ethereal Echoes in Midnight Blue

In the velvet night, we hear a sound,
Echoes of dreams, lost yet found.
The blue surrounds, a calming hue,
Wrapping our souls in a tranquil view.

Wisps of wonder drift on the air,
Carried by hope, light as a prayer.
Each whisper carries a tale to tell,
In the echoes, we fall under a spell.

Stars above sing a soft refrain,
Dancing shadows meet joy and pain.
Through the stillness, we trace our fears,
In the midnight blue, we shed our tears.

Here in this moment, we linger long,
Finding strength in a silent song.
As the universe wraps us tight,
We embrace our truths in the quiet night.

Fantasies Carried on Moonlit Waves

By the shore, where moonlight gleams,
Fantasies flow like whispered dreams.
The ocean breathes in silver light,
Painting our hopes, oh so bright.

Waves of wonder crash and play,
Carrying thoughts that drift away.
Each crest a memory made anew,
As hearts align with a cosmic view.

Beneath the tide, secrets rest deep,
In the silence, the world will keep.
With every ripple, desires swell,
In this dance, we hear their spell.

Moonlit tides guide our hearts to shore,
Opening paths to forevermore.
Together we float on dreams so grand,
In the twilight, we boldly stand.

Veils of Nebulae and Cloudy Fantasies

In the blush of dawn, veils unfold,
Nebulae shimmer with stories untold.
Clouds of thoughts drift in and out,
Painting the sky with whispers of doubt.

Colors blend in a cosmic dance,
Narrating tales of chance and romance.
Each veil a journey, a step unknown,
In the realms of dreams, we find our throne.

As stardust weaves through the morning glow,
Our fantasies rise, bright and slow.
Together we break through the misty gray,
Forging a path where hopes can sway.

With each inhale, the universe sings,
Filling our hearts with the light it brings.
In this expanse, we learn to trust,
Veils of wonder, in dreams we must.

Chronicles of the Night's Embrace

In shadows deep, the whispers sigh,
The moonlight dances, a silver tie.
Dreams unfold in velvet skies,
Secrets linger, where silence lies.

Night unveils her tender grace,
Stars illuminate the darkened space.
A canvas brushed with twinkling light,
Embraced in warmth, the heart takes flight.

With every heartbeat, moments flow,
Echoes of time, both fast and slow.
The world in slumber, spirits roam,
In night's embrace, we find our home.

Through echoes soft, the darkness calls,
A symphony as twilight falls.
In dreams, the soul may venture free,
Chronicles penned in mystery.

Wandering Among Celestial Pointers

Across the fields of endless night,
My thoughts take flight, a vivid sight.
The galaxies whisper, tales untold,
A tapestry woven in stars of gold.

Constellations guide the way,
A map of dreams where shadows play.
Each star a beacon, a distant call,
Wandering free, I feel it all.

The whispers of cosmos gently sway,
As I traverse the Milky Way.
With every step, I find my place,
In the dance of the universe's embrace.

Celestial pointers lead the heart,
In cosmic rhythms, we each take part.
Wandering far, yet feeling near,
The universe beckons, crystal clear.

Midnight's Gentle Reverie

In the hush of night, a sigh escapes,
Softly wrapped in twilight's shapes.
Whispers of dreams on gentle streams,
Filling the world with midnight's gleams.

Stars knit stories in silken threads,
While slumber cradles weary heads.
Each moment a lullaby, sweetly sung,
A tender hymn of the night, begun.

The world fades softly, shadows play,
In midnight's reverie, we drift away.
Thoughts take flight, like fireflies,
In the soft embrace of sleepy skies.

Midnight's grace, a soothing balm,
Holding us close, quiet and calm.
In this stillness, our spirits soar,
Bound by dreams forevermore.

Stars Dripping on Twilight's Canvas

As twilight spills on earth's warm skin,
The stars begin their dance, a spin.
Like droplets of light on a canvas spread,
Creating wonders, where dreams are bred.

Each star a brushstroke, soft and bright,
Painting the heavens with pure delight.
In twilight's glow, the world transforms,
In colors rich, beyond all norms.

The horizon swells with whispers sweet,
Beneath the sky, our hearts compete.
With every shade, a story weaves,
In twilight's grasp, the spirit believes.

As darkness yields to morning's grace,
The stars retreat, their rightful place.
Yet on this canvas, dreams remain,
Forever etched in twilight's reign.

Meditations Under a Canopy of Stars

Beneath the silent sky we lay,
Whispers of the night, soft and gray.
Dreams drift like clouds across the moon,
Time pauses here, a gentle tune.

Stars twinkle, secrets held so tight,
Drawing our souls into the night.
In this vastness, we find our peace,
A moment's joy, a sweet release.

Thoughts float like leaves on a stream,
Each a wish, each a dream.
Under this canopy, so wide and vast,
We share our stories, shadows cast.

The world fades into a subtle sigh,
As constellations dance, high in the sky.
Here in the dark, with hope's embrace,
We find our truth in this sacred space.

The Timeless Dance of Shadows

In the twilight's veil, we move and sway,
Shadows softly guide us on our way.
Each flicker tells a tale untold,
In the silence, our hearts unfold.

Whispers of the past brush by our ears,
Echoes of laughter, hidden fears.
We sway like branches in a gentle breeze,
In this dance of shadows, our spirits seize.

Under the watchful moon's silver gaze,
We twirl and twist through the night's haze.
The rhythm of time, elusive and bright,
In the dark we flourish, our limbs take flight.

As the stars blink down in quiet approval,
We lose ourselves in this timeless revel.
In each fleeting moment, we embrace the now,
The shadows our partners, with a solemn vow.

Notes from the Edge of Infinity

On the brink of a boundless sea,
Echoes of eternity call to me.
Whispers of time in the cosmic flow,
Carried by winds that softly blow.

Between the stars, a fleeting glance,
Life unfolds in a sacred dance.
Infinite dreams in the canvas of night,
Painting the dark with shimmering light.

Every heartbeat sings a cosmic song,
In this vast realm, we all belong.
Notes from the edge, sweetly they play,
Guiding us home, lighting the way.

In this embrace of the infinite grand,
We learn to hold what we cannot understand.
With souls intertwined, we climb so high,
At the edge of infinity, we learn to fly.

Unveiling Fantasies in the Night's Grasp

In the gloom, where shadows creep,
Fantasies awaken from their sleep.
Veils of dreams softly draw aside,
In these whispers, our hopes reside.

Stars ignite like sparks of fire,
Waking the heart's wildest desire.
Each moment spilling into the next,
The universe in beauty, complex and vexed.

Under the watch of the midnight sun,
Our imaginations race, unbound, they run.
With every heartbeat, a story unfolds,
In the night's grasp, our dreams take hold.

Together we wander through worlds unknown,
Unveiling the magic that we've outgrown.
In the silence, we dare to believe,
In the night's embrace, we learn to achieve.

Seraphim Dreams in the Quiet of Night

In the stillness, whispers soar,
Wings of light on heaven's floor.
Stars awaken, softly gleam,
Seraphim weave the night with dream.

Echoes of the sacred song,
Guiding spirits all along.
Gentle sighs and tender grace,
Cradle souls in warm embrace.

Veils of silver, shadows dance,
Underneath the moon's romance.
Lost in thoughts of pure delight,
Drifting deep in the velvet night.

As dawn approaches, dreams take flight,
Fading softly, out of sight.
Yet in hearts, the echoes keep,
Seraphim, in peace, we sleep.

Enchanted Trails of Light and Sound

Through the woods where silence reigns,
Whispers echo, love remains.
Footfalls softly brush the ground,
On enchanted trails, we are found.

Crickets call in rhythmic song,
As fireflies dance, bright and strong.
Moonlit paths, a silver thread,
Guiding dreams where wishes tread.

A melody of rustling leaves,
Weaving magic, the heart believes.
Nature's chorus sings so clear,
In the moment, all is near.

Whispers carry through the night,
In the forest, pure delight.
What we seek is here, profound,
On enchanted trails, love is found.

Radiant Glimmers of the Infinite

In the cosmos, sparks align,
Radiant glimmers, tales divine.
Each star a whisper from the past,
Infinite stories, unsurpassed.

Threads of light weave through the void,
Unraveled dreams, never destroyed.
Galaxies in dance command,
Eternal journeys, vast and grand.

Caught in wonder, eyes behold,
Timeless secrets yet untold.
Infinity's embrace so tight,
A dance of shadows, a dance of light.

With each heartbeat, we explore,
The essence of forevermore.
In radiant glimmers, we find peace,
Infinite love that will not cease.

Tidal Forces of the Dreamtime

Waves of thought crash on the shore,
Tidal forces, seek and soar.
In the depths, the dreams reside,
Ancient whispers, low and wide.

Oceans cradle hidden sights,
Guided by the moon's soft lights.
In the ebb and flow, we dive,
Sailing where the hopes alive.

Breath of currents, stories swell,
In the depths, all secrets dwell.
Each crest a journey, wild and free,
Tidal forces, calling me.

With every rise, the heart beats bold,
In the dreamtime, tales unfold.
Underneath the stars so bright,
Tidal forces, our delight.

Moments When the Cosmos Holds its Breath

In the hush of night, silence grows,
Stars shimmer softly, a gentle glow.
Time seems to linger, a frozen sigh,
As whispers of wonders drift by.

The moon bathes the world in silver light,
Dreams take flight in the velvet night.
Thoughts intertwine with the fabric of space,
In the stillness, we find our place.

Galaxies swirl, a celestial dance,
Each heartbeat echoes a cosmic chance.
In every twinkle, stories unfold,
Moments of magic in starlit gold.

The cosmos carries our hopes and fears,
In the quiet, we shed our mires.
Together we pause, just you and I,
Where time holds still, beneath the sky.

Flights of Fancy in the Stillness

Among the whispers of the dawn,
Imagination sings, pulling us along.
With every thought, we take to the air,
In this stillness, we wander with flair.

Feathers of dreams, they lift us high,
Painting the world with colors so spry.
In the quietude, our spirits roam,
Finding the wild within us, our home.

Clouds of cotton candy, skies of blue,
We chase the sun, in a dance so true.
The heartbeats echo as we glide,
On wings of fancy, we take our stride.

Moments stretched, like an endless road,
Finding the joy in each new ode.
With laughter and love as our guide,
In this stillness, we cannot hide.

Heavenly Palettes of Serenity

Brushstrokes of twilight paint the sky,
A canvas of dreams where colors lie.
Each hue whispers secrets of peace,
In this tranquil place, all troubles cease.

Soft pastels blend with deeper shades,
Nature's masterpiece, the night invades.
The stars awaken, a sparkling thread,
In this tranquil tapestry, we are led.

Gentle breezes caress the night air,
In every moment, we linger, we care.
The heart finds harmony in soft sounds,
As serenity blossoms, grace abounds.

With colors alive, and spirits free,
We dance in the shadows of the willow tree.
Life's gentle whispers, sweet melodies,
In this heavenly palette, we seize the breeze.

With Stars in Our Eyes and Hearts in Flight

Under a canopy of twinkling lights,
We dream of the cosmos, of mystical sights.
With stars in our eyes, we soar through the night,
Hearts filled with wonder, a boundless delight.

Every gleaming gaze is a wish afloat,
Navigating dreams on a silver boat.
Here, in this moment, our spirits ignite,
With stars in our eyes, we chase the light.

Laughter and joy weave through the air,
In the magic of night, we're free without care.
With hearts in flight, we dance and we sing,
Embracing the joy that each heartbeat brings.

The universe whispers its secrets untold,
In the vastness of night, we grow ever bold.
With stars in our eyes and love's guiding sight,
Together we journey, our spirits take flight.

Between Reality and Stardust

In the quiet glow of midnight air,
Dreams entwine with paths of stars.
Reality dances with a gentle flare,
Whispering secrets from afar.

In shadows cast by lunar beams,
Hope flickers like a fragile flame.
Through the fabric of our dreams,
We find a world that has no name.

Reality bows to magic's call,
As stardust weaves its golden thread.
In humble whispers, we stand tall,
Finding solace in what we've said.

Between the worlds, we spin and twirl,
In the garden where wishes thrive.
Stardust cradles every girl,
And boy, where all our dreams arrive.

The Lure of Incandescent Whispers

In twilight's hand, the secrets rest,
Incandescent whispers softly swirl.
They beckon hearts with hidden zest,
As shadows linger, thoughts unfurl.

Each word a spark, igniting flight,
Promises cradle the restless hours.
Underneath the blanket of night,
Whispers bloom like ephemeral flowers.

The moonlight dances on velvet skies,
Casting spells that feel so near.
As stardust twinkles in our eyes,
We're drawn into dreams without fear.

These whispers guide us on our way,
Through realms where only dreamers roam.
In incandescent hues, we sway,
Finding in darkness our true home.

Songs of Liberation in the Night Air

Beneath the stars, the music plays,
Echoes of freedom rise and soar.
With every note, the spirit sways,
In night's embrace, we yearn for more.

Voices blend in a gentle roar,
Breaking chains that held us tight.
As shadows dance on freedom's floor,
We sing our truths under the night.

Liberation sings in the breeze,
Whispers of courage fill the air.
With every breath, we feel the ease,
Embracing dreams without a care.

In harmony, we find our place,
United under the moon's gaze.
In every heart, a sacred space,
Where songs of freedom set ablaze.

Reflections of a Constellation's Heart

In the night sky, a story glows,
Reflections of dreams take their flight.
Each star a heartbeat, softly flows,
Guarding secrets through layers of light.

A constellation whispers clear,
Through the echoes of time and space.
In reflections, we hold them dear,
Finding solace in their embrace.

Every flicker, a tale untold,
In the silence, wisdom is found.
A tapestry of stars unfold,
Binding souls with a cosmic sound.

In the heart of the cosmic sea,
We glimpse the paths we've yet to trace.
Reflections guide us, wild and free,
Living within each star's warm grace.

Starlit Lullabies of the Wanderer

In the quiet night, whispers soar,
Dreams take flight, forever more.
Underneath the skies so vast,
Each twinkle speaks of journeys past.

The moonlight bathes the path I seek,
Guiding softly, gentle and meek.
Echoes of tales from stars above,
Wrapped in a blanket of endless love.

Footsteps linger in the cosmic dance,
Each moment a fleeting chance.
Voices of stardust call my name,
In the universe's wild, wondrous game.

Among the galaxies, I drift and roam,
In this celestial night, I find my home.
Starlit lullabies cradle my soul,
As I wander, searching to be whole.

The Journey of Wandering Souls

Roots once planted, now they fade,
On paths unknown, dreams cascade.
Hearts like compasses, pointing free,
Guided by hopes and reverie.

The winds of change whisper through trees,
Carrying thoughts upon the breeze.
Every step a story spun,
In the tapestry, we come undone.

Through valleys deep and mountains high,
We wander forth, beneath the sky.
Each soul a spark, a radiant flame,
Lost yet found, we're never the same.

With every sunrise, a chance to start,
To stitch together every heart.
The journey sings in cosmic tune,
As we dance beneath the watchful moon.

Floating Through Nebulous Realms

In cosmic clouds where colors blend,
We float and drift, time has no end.
Galaxies swirl in a dreamy haze,
Guiding our spirits through endless maze.

Stars like lanterns light the night,
Each shimmering story, pure delight.
Nebulas cradle our wayward dreams,
In their embrace, nothing is as it seems.

Together we wander the astral sea,
In search of worlds we long to see.
Every glance reveals a new dawn,
Adrift in wonder, forever drawn.

Curious souls in a dance so grand,
Unraveling secrets of the stars so planned.
Floating in realms where whispers gleam,
In nebula's heart, we chase our dream.

Celestial Ballet Beneath the Stars

Under the canopy, dancers twirl,
In the night's embrace, dreams unfurl.
Each movement echoes with grace and light,
As stars bear witness to the wondrous sight.

With every leap, we break the mold,
Stories of passion and love untold.
Galaxies pulse with the rhythm we share,
A celestial ballet, beyond compare.

Venus winks as we glide through space,
Communing with spirits in this timeless place.
Gravity's pull, a mere suggestion,
As we flow in the universe's direction.

In the night's hush, our souls align,
Twinkling with stardust, radiant shine.
Together we dance, eternal and free,
Beneath the vast stars, just you and me.